The Serious World

The Serious World

Poems

Laura Read

AMERICAN POETS CONTINUUM SERIES NO. 219

BOA EDITIONS, LTD. ◆ ROCHESTER, NY ◆ 2025

First Edition
23 24 25 26 7 6 5 4 3 2 1

Publications by BOA Editions, Ltd.—a nonprofit corporation under section 501 (c) (3) of the United States Internal Revenue Code—are made possible with funds from a variety of sources, including public funds from the Literature Program of the National Endowment for the Arts; the New York State Council on the Arts, a state agency; and the County of Monroe, NY. Private funding sources include the Max and Marian Farash Charitable Foundation; the Mary S. Mulligan Charitable Trust; the Rochester Area Community Foundation; the Ames Amzalak Memorial Trust in memory of Henry Ames, Semon Amzalak, and Dan Amzalak; and contributions from many individuals nationwide. See Colophon on page 95 for special individual acknowledgments. Any use of this publication to "train" generative artificial intelligence (AI) technologies to generate text is expressly prohibited.

Cover Design: Sandy Knight
Cover Art: Sandy Knight. Imagery created with photography by Hans Veth on Unsplash and Viktoriia on Adobe Stock
Interior Design and Composition: Isabella Madeira
BOA Logo: Mirko

BOA Editions books are available electronically through BookShare, an online distributor offering Large-Print, Braille, Multimedia Audio Book, and Dyslexic formats, as well as through e-readers that feature text to speech capabilities.

Cataloging-in-Publication Data is available from the Library of Congress.

BOA Editions, Ltd.
250 North Goodman Street, Suite 306
Rochester, NY 14607
www.boaeditions.org
A. Poulin, Jr., Founder (1938-1996)

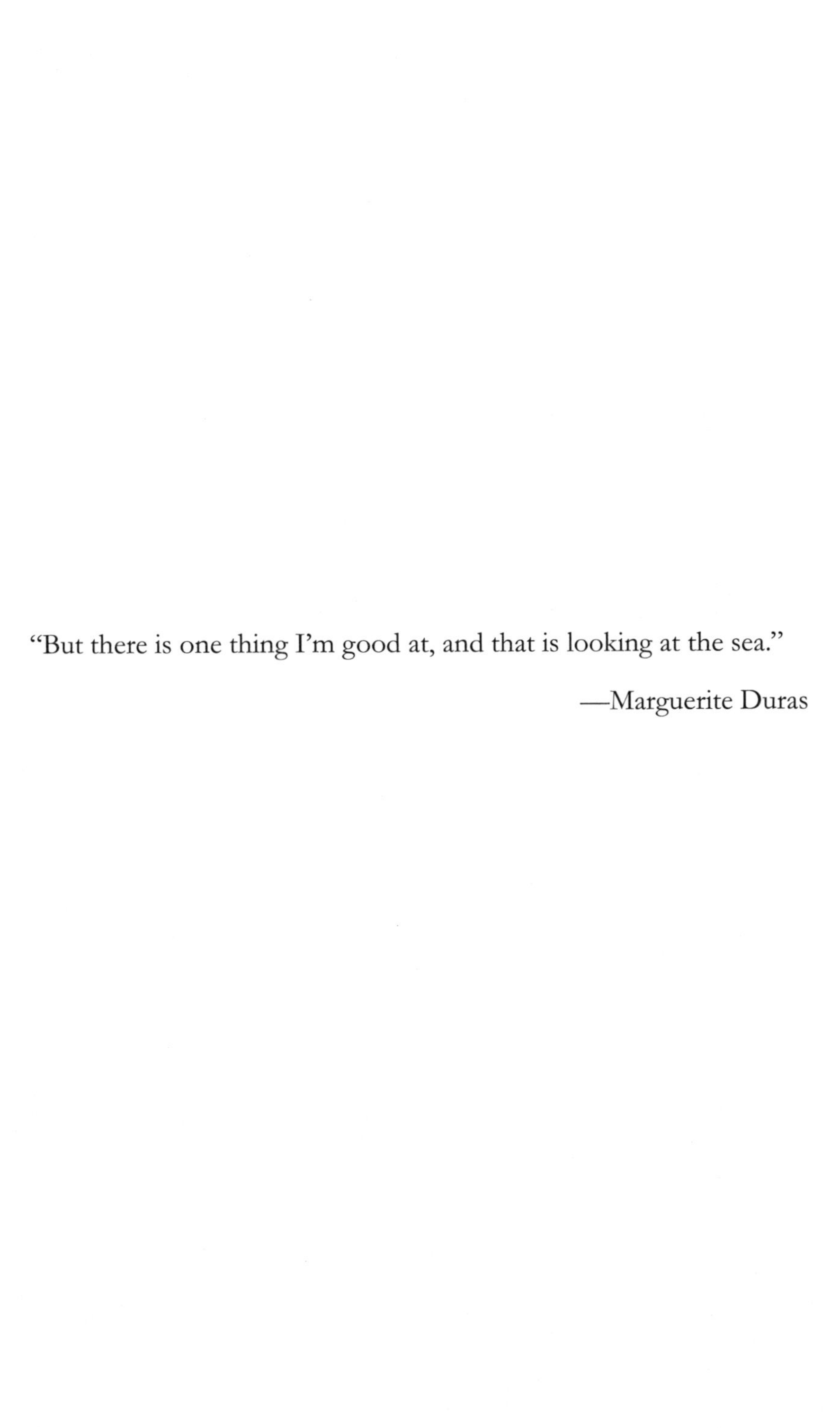

"But there is one thing I'm good at, and that is looking at the sea."

—Marguerite Duras

Contents

for Gail Reid-Gurian, 1957-2023
and Grace Abigail Wahlman, 1997-2024

and for the women who inspired these poems,
Sylvia Plath, Marguerite Duras, and Simone de Beauvoir

Mademoiselle Summer

I had one too, Sylvia,
I mean a summer in New York,
though I was only 9, and you were 21,

and you were writing for *Mademoiselle*
and I was only being called *mademoiselle*
by my grandpa who addressed me

as Mademoiselle Lorraine because
I wanted to go to France.
How did I invent this dream for myself?

I thought Paris was black and white
with splashes of pink. Something that's real
is that when Marie-Claire picked us up

from Charles de Gaulle, she definitely said,
Look out your windows for rabbits.
I was sitting on the floor of the van

she'd borrowed to pick up Les Americains,
but I got up on my knees to see all
the bunnies. I haven't eaten since Tuesday

because I have to have a colonoscopy.
It feels like floating in a light I think
you would call *blue and planetary.*

During my Mademoiselle summer,
my brother and I stayed three weeks
with our dead father's parents.

I had brought only one skirt
that I didn't know I'd be required
to draw lines of water over with an old

toothbrush every night and hang
in the bathroom while I showered
so that it would be wrinkle-free

for 8:00 a.m. mass, where I accompanied
Nanny while my brother and grandpa slept.
Apparently, men don't need to ask

for forgiveness. The skirt was white.
If I'd known, I'd have brought a different
one so I wouldn't have looked every morning

like an advertisement for purity,
a state you both desired (baths)
and despised (sex).

During your *Mademoiselle* summer,
you threw all your skirts out the window
of the Barbizan Hotel.

My grandfather was strange.
That's what people say when they don't want to
speak ill of the dead.

He used to cover up the television
with a sheet and then sit with us
on the plastic-covered couch until

we obliged him by laughing.
At every meal, he announced
that this was our home, which was frightening.

On the subway, Nanny pulled a roll
of saran wrap out of her purse
and wrapped me in it because I was cold.

Once on the street, she pointed at a man
and yelled, *That man wants to rape you!*
I felt sorry for the man who put his hands up

and fled. Perhaps he was Everyman, and this
was one of her lessons, but it felt too specific.
I have to say though that it stuck. Whenever

I see a man, I wrap myself in my grandmother's
invisible plastic. Once in the subway,
we saw a body. The police were taping off

the area. There was blood around the head.
It was like our trip to Brooklyn in 1979
had been written to be written. Like the summer

of 1953 when you began to break down.
Today I am hungry in a way
that makes me realize I have never been hungry.

On the last day of fourth grade, my teacher told us
she was moving to Australia.
I went home and flung myself down on my bed

and cried without thinking, *I'm going to cry now*,
and thought, *Oh so all that other crying was made up?*
This is finally it? Mrs. Welch?

Dear Sylvia,

When I was 32, I was driving home from work
on Sunset Boulevard, which sounds more picturesque

than it is: there's an old coffee shop that is sometimes
an ice cream shop and is now boarded up,

and a bar called Lucky You.
Railroad tracks that look like relics except

that a train is always coming, persistent
as history, so the rattling is part of the background

of every thought I've ever had
in my little car on the way to and from

my job, which was sometimes all the time
and space in a day when I could *hear my own thoughts*,

as my mother used to say when I asked her why
she stayed up so late and was always tired.

This day when I was 32, I heard my own thoughts.
They were saying, *When you get home,*

there might be enough time to take the boys
to the park before you make dinner.

They were saying I should grade at least ten
essays before bed. Then again, park, dinner, essays.

And then, why is there so much ringing?
And then, what they call a breakthrough,

as I took the turn by where Lucky You
is now but wasn't then,

Maybe it's not like this for everyone.
Maybe I shouldn't tell you this,

but my husband used to say I was having
a Sylvia Plath day when he came home

from work and I left him immediately
with the children. I know you are not a joke,

but when you're dead, this is one of the things
you can become.

I don't know if you had the repeating.
Or the ringing. But I know the electroshock

made it so that any frightening thought Esther had
would *swing loose like a noose*,

which is what I like about
selective serotonin reuptake inhibitors.

When I was 32, I went to a therapist named Linda
who wore the quiet kind of clogs that said

she was comfortable with herself.
There were certain things she was okay with me

feeling and other things she wasn't,
which felt like home.

Her office had a loveseat and a picture of her son,
and remembering this made me sad when I read

her obituary a few years ago.
She fired me, which I found strange.

Said she'd done all she could.
This also felt familiar, so I shrugged and went.

I was 35 by then. I found another therapist
in my 40s. She also had some things she'd listen to

and some things she wouldn't.
When I tried to tell my mother I'd had sex,

she put her hand up between us.
How did she know? I hadn't said anything yet!

Am I always about to say something upsetting
to mothers and therapists? Are my thoughts

that transgressive and transparent?
Sylvia, I don't think we would have liked each other

in Real Life, which is something we say now.
In Real Life, I prefer women who have been

as conditioned as I have. I don't want to do
all the procuring of actual and figurative drinks.

But in print, I want a woman who tells
the truth. Who resists. Who knows

when the hospital serves green beans
with baked beans that they're messing with her.

Everyone knows you don't eat
two kinds of beans together.

The Gambler

I called my mother to say,
I hope you're not going out, and she said,
Well, I do still go to the clubhouse,
but my allergies are bad.
Oh, her ordinary allergies!
I can see her eyes streaming and feel
her irritation emanating from the sink
where she washes the dinner dishes
regardless. I say, *You can't believe*
how eerie it is to live in this town without you,
especially now. I don't say this.
Instead, I ask about Kenny Rogers
and how she's taking his death.
She says, and of course she knows this,
Well, he's had dementia for years.
And then, proud of her own cleverness,
she tells me that Kenny
really knew when to fold them.
So I tell her my own Gambler story,
how after I read the news,
I called my son, even though he was just
upstairs, and sang, *On a warm summer's evening,*
and he joined in, *On a train bound for nowhere.*
I hadn't thought how far we would get,
but the song is so good,
so the Gambler and Matthew and I
took turns a-starin' out the window at the darkness.
I like it when the Gambler says,
Son, I've made a life out of readin' people's faces
because then Matthew is the son
and I am the Gambler,
and I *have* made a life out of this.
I think that's how far we got
when Matthew said, *Wait, why are we doing this?*
and I said, *Oh, because Kenny Rogers died,*

which I had in fact forgotten,
and Matthew gasped,
Mom, how could you do that?
You made me so happy
and then so sad.

I Had Trouble in Getting to Solla Sollew

It's weird to know you're going on a trip, that it's
inevitable and won't be pleasant but might also be
miraculous, and not know when.

My younger friends have been waiting for news.
The first thing I tell them is that at the end,
you bleed all the time.

(I asked my older friend, who has already been,
and she said, *Oh yes, that's a sign.*)
The only other thing I've learned so far

is that you have to lay out three pairs of pajamas
at night for "costume changes," as my husband
calls them. The sweat starts at your hairline.

It reminds me of the Play-Doh barbershop toy
I used to have where you turned a crank
on the side of the tiny person and the Play-Doh

hair started growing through the holes in his head.
This amuses me in the night when I'm toweling off
and shivering. The whole thing is a lot like

being twelve when all the girls in my class
were waiting and we knew who had gotten it
and who hadn't and I spent the night at Miriam's

and she showed me her diary which she could literally
unlock and how she had decorated the day she got it
with stickers. I got mine when I was thirteen,

which meant Miriam had an invisible power
over me, like the power I have over you
right now. Which is interesting since I'm losing

my power. Or that is the story I'm being told.
Actually, I've been told very little.
Miriam and I knew more about what was about

to happen to our bodies than I know now.
I tried asking my doctor some of my many questions.
Do hormones cause cancer? Do people still take them?

What is excessive bleeding? Isn't all bleeding
excessive? How long will the whole thing last?
She laughed hard at that one.

About the hormones, she said, *We'll cross that bridge*
when we come to it. Well, of course we will,
it's a bridge and we have to keep going,

but I'd like some more information on how
the bridge crossing is going to go down.
Lately, I've been thinking about

I Had Trouble in Getting to Solla Sollew.
The narrator stubbed his toe so he decided
to leave his country and try to get to Solla Sollew

where such things would not happen,
but he had so many troubles along the way
that he was able to teach all children

not to run from their problems.
I loved Solla Sollew.
The harder it was to get there, the more

I wanted to go. The landscape was desert
and feathery bushes and sudden cliffs,
and a pink bridge that curved upward

covered with pink canopies shaped
like wishbones and all of it looked like
it had just been drawn.

Griselda

When Ann and I were young,
she would pick me up for school
in her green Buick
which she'd named Griselda,
and I would always have to put
my mascara on in the car,
and she would say,
Why can't you be on time, even once?
Bruce Hornsby was singing,
Listen to the mandolin rain,
and it was actually raining,
and Griselda was driving through it,
low and wide like a boat,
and Ann's mom was at home,
being alive.

Duras

I like when people list all the things
they're not good at. Like Esther,

who can't cook or do shorthand or choose
a fig from all the figs.

Or Marguerite Duras, who tries
to be like other people and go to the beach

but then gets there late
because she always ends up doing things

by halves. It's that bit of toughness
that knows better.

Like when I was 26 and my mother
did not approve of me moving home

from Washington, D.C., where I never
felt comfortable because those buildings

were not my buildings and I couldn't feel
just where the river was from my bed.

And also because I was in love with a man
who said it was okay to love where you're from

and not always be leaving and who was himself
quite tall and broad-shouldered and a sort

of shelter and took me to the lake
where I'd grown up swimming and worked

for two years as a camp counselor, carrying canoes
and supervising children and getting up early

and walking up the steepest hill to the unit
for sixth graders, the age I like best

because they are children still but on their way
out, so they have that kind of wisdom

a poem has when it can turn back and see
there was something just there, in the shadows.

The other night I was at the restaurant
I'd always wanted to go to because I like the way

the lights drape over the patio.
My friend asked me why I had not done

what my family wanted and if I knew
I was the outsider and understood the irony

of my quiet devotion and my invisible rebellion.
And then I did.

When Marguerite Duras was dying,
Yann Andréa asked her what she had to say

for herself, a question my mother
asked me often as a child,

and Duras just said, "Duras."
Her name is so obdurate and durable

that it makes the answer work at many levels,
one of them silent but revolutionary,

the way the stones you can see at the bottom
of the river between miles seven and eight

on the trail where I like to ride my bike
and stop and sit on my bench and drink

my water and eat my granola bar
are so large and clear and thoughtless.

Appearance vs. Reality

Félix Vallotton's ten woodcuts
called "Intimacies" look at first like actual
intimate moments.

For example, a man is holding
a woman who is whispering something in his ear.
But it's called *The Lie.*

My high school English teacher Mr. Griffin
used to say that Appearance vs. Reality
was the theme for every story.

He underlined *appearance* and *reality*
with great emphasis. This made me want to find
a story that did not contain this theme,

which has become a lifelong and futile quest.
Once poor Mr. Griffin fell out of his chair.
He was sitting at his desk and had just

put his head down for a minute
while we were taking a test,
and he must have drifted off, and the chair

he was sitting in had wheels and rolled back,
and he fell and came up from behind the desk
red-faced. He appeared to be mortified,

and he was. It was such a genuine moment.
Later that year when we studied Emily Dickinson's
"I like a look of Agony," I thought of

Mr. Griffin's face after his fall.
Because I know it's true.
The difficult thing about Vallotton's woodcuts,

and most of life, is that what is true
is often hidden, as Mr. Griffin said.
I like that too. It's a challenge.

What's the lie? The thing that is whispered?
The family life of the bourgeoisie?
The embrace itself?

Vallotton liked to work "from black to white
...[pulling] his subjects out of the darkness,"
leaving so much we can't see.

Sometimes, as in "The Money," this is everything
except for the couple standing at the window.
In "The Irreparable," it is the space

between the couple who sit together
on their couch, looking out at us instead of
at each other. I have been lied to

and felt thrilled at the moment when I saw the lie
for what it was. Irreparable.
I spent the last six years believing someone

loved me because he sent me cryptic stories
about a woman who could have been me
but wasn't. I spent hours each day choosing

the pain of hoping and wondering over
the pain of my children growing up
and my husband and I growing older

and the sorrow settling everywhere like a fine
dust you don't have the strength to keep dusting.
It was another woman, after all.

So obvious. And yet I missed it.
Once Mr. Griffin told my parents that I had more
talent in my little finger—and here he held up

his own—than he had in his whole body,
which he gestured at. I've never forgotten this,
not just because it was a nice compliment

but also because of his willingness to draw
attention to his own body
just to give me this gift.

Maybe I Just Don't Like Biographies

I never had a "platinum summer," Sylvia,
never sunbathed in a white swimsuit until my hair
was blonde and my skin tan
(I have red hair and freckles),
never ate oysters by the sea with boys
I'd grown up with who'd become eligible men.
Do I need to know about every boy you ever dated?
(Does it make sense to envy the dead?
Does it have to make sense?)
What I do like is knowing that your mom
and Helen Vendler's mom were friends,
that they pushed you and Helen side by side
in your strollers, that we know now
who you and Helen grew up to be,
but that you were just ordinary babies then.
Were the strollers actually prams?
I had a pram. It was navy blue and had a plastic
window that I saw 1970 through.
You did not see 1970, and I have so many feelings
for you that this makes me sad.
When you and Helen were in your prams,
it was 1933. You saw leaves above you,
your eyes, older than Helen's, studying their shapes
(spades, hands) and their shades of green
(pine, fern), feeling for them in the dark of your mind
before language. In 1997,
I visited St. Patrick's Cathedral in Dublin
and saw the gold basin where Jonathan Swift
was baptized. Jonathan Swift! You remember him!
Imagine the priest pouring the water over baby

Jonathan and thinking he had changed him.
Imagine him not knowing that baby contained
Gulliver's Travels and *A Modest Proposal*
or how a corner of the church would be dedicated
to him, a glass case where they keep his early
writings, his death mask, and his actual skull
from when, ninety years after his death, they exhumed
his body and found a loose bone in his inner ear.
This is how we know (though he never did)
that what looked like insanity was in fact
Ménière's Disease, the symptoms of which
include a ringing in the ear
that can sound like voices.

Not Ideal

I am trying to remember what my face
used to look like

so I can draw it on.
I am trying to decide if I'm really

at work or if this whole thing
is imagined. The only lights on

in the building are the ones
that come on when you walk into a room.

I walk into so many rooms
for their silent applause. It's weird

how you have to keep moving.
Periodically, I have to get up from my desk

and walk around or just accept
the dark. It's usually best

to accept things. My office-mate once
untangled my phone cord and asked me why

I hadn't. I realized something important
about myself then. I do circle my eyes

in eyeliner and draw on my eyebrows
and straighten my hair and pluck

the mole above my lip even though
it will be under my mask.

Once I asked my son if the mole
was unsightly, and he replied that it was

Not Ideal. So now when something
is Not Ideal, I point at my upper lip.

I sleep a lot, but I'm always tired.
After I teach in my mask, my throat hurts,

and I have to lie down when I get home.
I feel the way I used to feel

when I was pregnant and my body was making
another body and needed to concentrate.

I lie in my bed under my wool blanket
but not under all the covers.

Because I'll be back in it again soon,
and I want it to feel different.

It is dangerous to wrap yourself in the sheet of someone else's life

is something someone wrote about you,
Sylvia, because I am not
alone in my feelings for you,

a fact which fills me with jealousy or rather
feels like the small piece of banana bread
I choked on the other night and couldn't quite

cough loose so that it woke me and my sons
rushed upstairs to pound on my back
while my husband slept.

Sometimes on long walks, my makeup runs,
and I look like Courtney Love,
who is famous for being the wife of Kurt Cobain.

You can visit his cardigan in a museum.
The way you can visit your braid
in a library in Indiana or your Girl Scout uniform

and your senior thesis on doubles in Dostoevsky
in an exhibit at the Smithsonian.
People thought his sadness was beautiful,

bronzed by his death. I'm sure you understand.
Courtney had a band named Hole, an album
called *Live Through This*. Written before

Kurt's suicide. We always think we've lived through
a lot when in fact it's just starting.
I always thought the picture on that album cover

was Courtney Love, but actually it's a model
dressed as a prom queen holding a bouquet
and wearing a crown, her lipsticked

mouth open and her mascara smeared
in a way that can't be overlooked.
Courtney Love might be one of my doubles.

I know you don't agree, but that's because
we just met. Matthew said the banana bread felt like
it should have walnuts in it but didn't.

He said I choked on an invisible walnut.
The other day, I was on a panel
for a literary festival

called Unmaking the Patriarchy of the Mind.
I leaned in close to the microphone
as I answered the question about how my work

is changing as I get older.
I said, *I think I'm getting angrier*,
but my smile wouldn't quit.

Totally

You know how the dead are.
They refuse to be criticized.
Like now when I think of the way Grace
used to say *Totally*
whenever I said something with which she identified,
I have to be solidly endeared and none percent annoyed.
You know how the young are.
They land on a word, and use it in more circumstances
than it was intended for.
Actually, it's surprising how much she said *Totally*
when in fact it was a word we used when I was young
before she was born.
Totally, for example, goes with *tubular*.
You would never say *tubular* on its own.
It goes with leg warmers and silver bracelets up your whole arm
and hairsprayed bangs and Madonna singing
"Get into the Groove" in *Vision Quest*,
which was (totally) filmed here in Spokane in 1985.
Anyone who grew up here in the 80s loves the scene
where Matthew Modine runs over the Monroe St. Bridge
to Journey's "Only the Young." We loved how clearly
you could see in that scene that that was the town
where we (totally) lived.
My friend Ann loves Journey. She was *just a small town girl /*
living in a lonely world. Now, as an adult, she says
she recognizes they weren't very good,
but that's the thing, isn't it? There are things you know
when you're young and things you know
when you're old.
And what if you're dead by then?
The chorus of that song just repeats "Only the young can say"
until it runs out of notes.
Mostly, I liked the way Grace said *Totally*.
There is nothing more total than death,
I want to say to her now. I want to say, *You're gone,*

Grace, like totally, like a Total Eclipse
or your total is. Totally means I agree with you completely,
so much that I want to exclaim
because I've felt the way you just described.
In fact, you helped me understand it,
and now we're both less alone,
which is exciting, isn't it? Had you been alive
when we arrived, this is what
I would have said.

The Serious World

I have a Philosophy teacher named Theodra
who lives in Philadelphia. I can only see her

in the small box on Zoom,
but I have made a thorough study nonetheless.

I like how she seems to be lying back in her chair
or perhaps in bed. She hasn't been feeling well lately,

so I'm glad she can teach while resting her body,
which I've learned from her is not a facticity.

Theodra has addressed this as well—
well, it's really Simone de Beauvoir, but coming to me now

through Theodra—"It's a tragedy to be a child."
And also, we can't be happy because we were once children.

Yes, I knew this. I have always been a great Philosopher,
it turns out. What I didn't know is that it's an issue

of Freedom. As children, we are pre-Subjectivity,
which means we don't yet understand we have a self.

I had a porcelain angel on the table by my bed.
She had wings I accidentally broke off, which I viewed

as an improvement. She had a porcelain puppy.
Has. She still sits on the headboard behind me.

She is a facticity. She was there in the room I had
when my father was still alive. You can't change that.

But my body is not. Look at it. It's not so bad.
I can go ahead and let it out of the yard

and see what it does. I can assign it a different meaning.
Look at these new lines sweeping back

under my eyes. I like them. They look like wings.
Not the wings of an angel but of a large bird,

the kind that just keep on opening.
We can't be happy because we were children,

and that means we used to live in a world
that someone else made for us, the napkin folded

under the fork, the pansy in the center of the plate.
And now what? How do we relate to our freedom?

A Subman will just do what they're told. A Serious Man
lives in the Serious World to which we've all

been assigned. Gets a job and a house and a wife
and 2.5 children. Accepts, like a child,

these readymade values. We all live
in this Serious World, and one way to do it

is to get a set of plates with pansies in the middle
and set the same table. I do not blame The Serious Man

for his conformity, or the Subman either,
for that matter—it is hard to get your head around

Freedom, as they say. It's like folding a fitted sheet,
which eventually you have to just stuff in the drawer.

And then there's Nihilism—if everything is human-made,
then nothing has meaning. I don't want to make

all the meaning myself. Theodra says this is a choice,
that all of these are choices, except for those living

in pre-Subjectivity, the Child and the Oppressed.
You can also be an Adventurer, but this means

your projects are fun but empty of transcendence
(*Think Colonists, Bros, Nazis, Venture Capitalists*).

The problem here is a lack of thought for the Other
who also has Freedom, which can be inconvenient.

And then The Individual which of course
we all hope to be and Theodra says we can.

She says these are types, not real people,
and we move between them all the time.

She says it's not like she looks at one of her neighbors
and thinks *There goes the Subman!* (She's funny like that.)

The Individual knows that he has Freedom
and that I do too. Thank you, Individual!

He acknowledges the ambiguity of ethics
and the facticity of the past. (*What?* Or *What the Fuck?*

which is another thing Theodra says.)
I like it when Theodra asks a question and then

takes a sip of her tea and waits
like we're in grade school.

I wait right back at her like I never did then.
I have that Freedom, and I know it now.

Before Whistler

Before we even sat down at the table
after not sitting down at any table together
for more than twenty years,

Jen said, *I thought you were mad at me about Eric.*
This was the first of many startling things.
One was the fact that our Thai salads came

as only a bed of lettuce with chicken pieces
buried like secrets underneath,
and we had to ask for the other toppings

listed on the menu, and the server sullenly
brought a small bowl of almonds
and julienned carrots and green onions.

It's hard to know what it's okay to ask for.
In the hours we sat there watching the dark
cover the river and fill the windows,

Jen told me the story of her marriage,
the years of watching her husband drink
away time, something we all want to get rid of

and hold on to, and she apologized
for this too, saying she hoped it had not
brought back painful memories of Eric,

whose other qualities had been obscured
by his addiction and what he had done to me
in that little white house in which Jen and I

lived together our senior year of college.
But it was only a year. Not a marriage.
Jen showed me a picture of our house,

which is gone now,
so when I walk by the grass where it was,
the wildflowers that grew up around

our front windows are just ghosts
of wildflowers that you can choose
to believe in or not.

My eyes go to the garage, which is where I lived.
I chose it because it had its own entrance
and I wanted the freedom to come and go,

without anyone knowing, because I like it
when one hand does not know
what the other is doing.

I had not thought how cold it would be
to sleep in a garage,
how my boyfriend would have to seal

the windows in plastic with a hair dryer
and even then I would need two space heaters
and a hat to sleep.

Jen shows me a picture of me, turning my head
in surprise at being photographed
because I am only vacuuming.

I'm wearing that black angora sweater
I liked even though it made me feel guilty
about the bunnies. Why is there a crucifix

on the wall? How holy were we?
And there's the couch with the green
and peach pillows and the very small television

on which all my roommates watched
Days of Our Lives at lunch while I went
with my boyfriend to the cold garage.

Jen is talking, and I am walking back
through that house, taking things out
of the garage and handing them to her,

things I think she might want.
Like the time right after we graduated
when she broke up with her boyfriend

on the phone just after he'd given her a ring
with a ruby and a diamond.
She told him he had been a crutch

while she rocked vigorously in our wicker
rocking chair, like Whistler's mother
might have done when she was young.

When my boyfriend broke up with me
and I watched him walk out the door
of my garage for the last time, I wept for days.

I tried to be quiet, but once, I told Jen,
I opened the bathroom door after a shower,
and she had left me note and a muffin

on a pretty plate, did she remember?
She did not.
Take it, I said, and the time we trespassed

and swam in the pool of this very hotel
and got caught and ran through the parking lot,
soaking wet and laughing,

and the ‘60s party when we all wore turquoise
dresses, and the nights she spent
at the art studio drawing beautiful hands

in charcoal, and her own hands, which we called
her old hands because they were wrinkled
even then.

Infinity

Sylvia, I thought you might be interested to know
what we've done with therapy.

We've dispensed with electroshock
and lobotomies, but we still like talking.

And we have EMDR—
Eye Movement Desensitization and Reprocessing.

There are different ways to do it,
but the way I did it with Gail was with a screen

on which little red dots of lights moved
back and forth at a certain speed (24)

and in a certain pattern (infinity).
I had to watch the lights and think about

the room I slept in when I was six.
Oh, I can see your eyes moving now

under your dead lids.
You're thinking of your room, aren't you?

How your father was still alive.
Still had his leg.

My room had a picture on the wall
of a girl leaning her head on God's giant hand.

A stuffed camel on the floor, legs splayed.
The gray dresser with the brass handles

that clanged when you opened the drawers.
The patchwork sheets and the Raggedy Ann

bedspread on the bed that was always made
unless I was in it.

There you go. Now watch the lights.
Stop. How do you feel?

I tried to pick the camel up
but he couldn't stand, and there was no way

to arrange him neatly on the floor to hide this fact.
If you had lived to be old,

you could have sat on Gail's loveseat
and watched the lights and visited the rooms

where you felt the worst and yes, I admit
that doesn't sound good, but the lights

are a Giant Eraser, Sylvia, the long white kind
that worked better on chalk than the small gray ones,

the kind the teachers used at the end of the day,
dragging them carefully from one end of the board

to the other while I took the gray felt ones outside
and banged them on the side of the building

because I couldn't bear to watch.
This is EMDR. You could have lived past

everything, had it been invented.
This kind of thing makes me mad.

Had my dad lived a little longer, they could have
saved him: we know so much more now

about kidneys. But he didn't.
I just thought you should know

you were on the right track.
I mean, with your poems.

You have to keep going back to the rooms,
you have to say how you feel.

All you needed was Gail and the lights.
I like the infinity pattern.

My friend Ann is frightened of infinity.
I expect you are not.

So much gold in the bank

I went to see my mother to help her
look for the letter my father wrote to her
when he was dying.
We sorted through all the plastic bins,
found my mom's dissertation and my dad's,
discovered that Dad's was much shorter,
so she won that round.
Which reminded me of when my husband
was talking about how his brother
always won everything, and I saw
the look in our sons' eyes that said,
Well, you outlived him.
There were envelopes full of letters
of condolence, an embroidery of a bear
I had made that said *This bears my love to you.*
He is holding a heart. I asked my mother
why he was in storage.
How did she know where my love was
without him? There was my dad's famous
olive shirt with the tan stripes,
which I started buttoning to see
how slight he was. It felt so ordinary
like all those Sunday nights my mother and I
folded clothes in front of the TV.
We found the letter in the last envelope
which contained his wallet with pictures of us
in the little plastic sleeves, his will,
and a leather key chain embossed with flowers
that made me feel a great fondness.
The letter was the last thing in the envelope.
It said *Jane* in his handwriting,
and when I handed it to her, she was happier
than I'd ever seen her.
You have so much gold in the bank with me, she said
when I was leaving, and I felt good everywhere

though I didn't deserve it,
but no one deserves what they get.

I was just inside a poem

The pieces were everywhere, like torn blossoms,
as I walked across the campus of the university
where I grew up because my mother taught there
and where I myself went and where today I returned
as a guest speaker to room 314, the classroom
where I once wrote on the board and pretended
I was a teacher. I looked in my mother's office,
room 311, but she wasn't there.
After class, Ann and I walked across campus
like it was 1992, but our house where we lived then
has been torn down. Ann is a professor,
and I am a poet, and we are who we wanted to be,
and this is how it's all turned out. The End.
But some guy is still blasting music from DeSmet,
the all boys' dorm where my college boyfriend lived,
and I wanted to yell up, *Hey BJ, turn it down.*
Yeah, that was his actual name. Sometimes I say
it didn't mean that then, but it did.
Why do these boys think we should all listen to the music
they like? It used to be "Sweet Home Alabama."
Now it's "Somebody That I Used to Know."
You can get addicted to a certain kind of sadness. Amen.
We walked by a couple kissing on the lawn
and doing that thing where they pull apart from each other
while still holding hands so they can pull each other back.
The girl said, "Oh you have an eyelash," and brushed
the boy's cheek. During class, a student asked me
if I always think of myself as a woman when I write
or if I'm ever androgynous. I said, *Always* and *Never.*
This made me sad. I wonder who I might be
had I not lived so long in this culture, going to the kind
of parties one girl in class talked about
at the Baseball House, the male gaze following me
everywhere from the open window on the third floor
of DeSmet, from St. Aloysius's two spires.

I don't think we said *male gaze* back then,
but you don't need words for feelings
in order to have them, as we know from Childhood.

The Woman in Love

Sylvia, I just want you to know that even though
I am sometimes bored by the 900 pages
of your short life, I did tell my philosophy class

about you in my presentation on Beauvoir's
Woman in Love. I put that picture of you
in your white dress looking to the side

like study had caught you up in its arms
for a moment and you had forgotten
yourself on my PowerPoint and explained

that you were a case in point of what Beauvoir
said girls wanted and realized they couldn't have,
which is why they attach themselves to men.

You said men always thought women wanted
to seduce them when actually
women wanted to be them,

wanted "to sleep in an open field,
to travel west, to walk freely at night."
This cleared up so much.

I have spent many years like Victor Hugo's mistress
waiting for him in the apartment where he kept her
(in a pumpkin shell!), writing him thousands

of letters. He saw her so little that "even
when the littles added up, they were very little."
And her name was Juliette! Drouet!

Did she know she was a poem? I do.
Juliette said "the woman in love
is like a squirrel in a cage."

You would have liked her, at least for a while.
I put a picture of a squirrel in a cage
on my PowerPoint, and people laughed silently

in their little Zoom boxes.
Then I showed them the April squirrel
on my 2021 Squirrel Calendar.

She is standing in a field of wildflowers,
lifting one up and yelling at it
with a grand exuberance.

Confused Dog

The summer after Grace died,
I couldn't read. I'd lie in bed with my books
but look at dog memes on my phone instead.
I had a particular dog I liked—
you can google Confused Dog meme and find him,
and you can even buy a print of him on Etsy,
which I might. I loved all the different scripts
people wrote about what he might be thinking.
I do like to imagine what dogs are thinking.
I have a voice I do for my dog Henry
when he addresses my husband.
All his sentences start with *Well, Brad,*
because he is exasperated at how little
Brad understands him.
Eventually, I read a short book called
Absolutely and Forever
about a character named Marianne
who spent years pining
for a character named Simon,
years which she described as being
in the Love Asylum.
I liked this and chewed on it slowly
as I could only handle one idea at a time.
Then I read *The Inseparables*, a lost novel
of Simone de Beauvoir's, and it was just
the story of her friendship with Zaza
that I'd already read in her memoir
but with their names changed to Sylvie and Andrée.
I liked thinking about how parts of the story
revealed themselves differently
in fiction. But really I wanted to think
of one thing only
and I chose Sylvie's first impression
of Andrée in which she said that if you said
the words *peach* or *orchid* to her, she would shiver

and break out in gooseflesh.
Imagine being that sensitive, I say to my dog,
who is confused and cannot imagine this.
My favorite thing the Confused Dog discusses
is math. I love it when they put him in a classroom
filled with pencils and desks and he gets the wrong
answer, an answer so wrong you can't fathom
how he came up with it. I also like when he's on a plane
and the pilot is talking, and he can't make out
the words so he thinks they're going to crash.
This is how I feel all the time, I want to tell him.
It's hilarious.

Love Poem with Staples

After the nurse has taken all the staples
out of Brad's new scar, he asks me how many
there were, and I regret not counting,

but I looked away,
which is my privilege,
the way I can go on walks and he can't,

or drive to the lake and swim for a few hours
and come home with my arms freckled.
This is the seventh surgery

since his accident fifteen years ago,
the hardest except for the first
because the doctor had to rebreak

the bone and start over.
We can rebuild him, we have the technology
is something Brad likes to say

because before all this,
he was a boy in the 1970s
who watched *The Six Million Dollar Man.*

The morning of the accident, our sons
were at swim lessons.
I was watching Matthew's

round head as he did his bobs, the water
slicking his hair to his face so he looked like
he was being born.

I never saw him like this since I had c-sections
and my own staples,
so I couldn't get enough.

One of my last memories of Brad's brother
happened at Staples.
They were leaving to drive across the country,

and we were saying goodbye, and it was late
and dark, but they were still going
to try to make it to Montana,

and of course before they left,
they needed to print something
for a church service or something

because for them time
was always something you could make more of
which made me purse my lips

with an older-than-my-years impatience
because time exists.
We said goodbye under the red sign

that said Staples, and this stapled itself
to the moment so now when I drive by Staples,
I think of Terry bending down to hug me

for one of the last times before he died.
When we went in the room
to have Brad's staples removed,

he told me this was where he was
when he learned about Terry.
For his follow-up appointment for Surgery 3.

That he listened to his sister-in-law's voicemail
in the bathroom and then told them
at the front desk he had to go.

He walked into the room
on the same crutches he'd been using
since the original accident.

The handles are wrapped in blue tape,
and parts of the gray cushions are flecking off.
They are the Velveteen Rabbit of crutches.

There are many ways to be broken,
and Brad is all of them.
After she was dead too,

I read in my mother-in-law's journal
how grateful she was for me
so Brad would not be alone.

I thought how prescient because now
it's just me here with him, and the nurse
who is funny and kind and fills up

the room and makes us feel like things
will be all right but is also almost done
with the staples and on her way out.

The Girl of '91

I said I had to be the first to go through
that gate, to sit on the porch with Mary Ruefle
and welcome Old Age on her tiny feet,

but no, I'm still standing with Mary
at the open freezer
in the middle of the night, holding bags

of mixed vegetables to my neck.
What even are mixed vegetables?
They taste like their shapes and colors, like maybe

they were made by preschoolers.
In preschool, I learned *peninsula* and *isthmus.*
We made their shapes out of clay and left them

to dry on paper plates.
When I think of land jutting out into water,
I think of this wet clay.

Annie Ernaux is very concerned
with the girl she was in 1958.
She is different enough from her now

that she calls her The Girl of '58.
Usually I wonder what I know now
that I didn't then, but perhaps it is the other way

around: I just had to look up *isthmus* and *peninsula*
to make sure I was picturing
them correctly, and if you must know,

I hadn't remembered that an isthmus
is continually connected to land,
which is comforting, to be connected by at least

a narrow strip to where you began.
Annie Ernaux points out that the Girl of '58
knew more math than the woman she became,

as did my Girl of '91. I want to tell
Annie of 2014 about the Girl of '91
and the room she had in France

which was entirely white like Purity itself,
and how the Girl of '91 had a square bottle
of Ralph Lauren Eau de Toilette

that was burgundy,
which she set on a white shelf so her eyes
always flew right to it when she walked in.

At first, when I skipped a period,
I thought of the quiet linen closet
where my mother hid the maxi pads and the blue

towels in that bathroom
with the starburst patterns and the Ivory soap
my stepdad liked that cracked

and cleaning that tub on Saturdays
and soaking in it sometimes and shaking
baby powder over my clean skin

because I liked the smell and then
going to bed to dream of being the Girl of '91
who is still alive and wants someone

to remember how that red bottle
looked against the white,
how delightful it is to disrupt expectation.

Like Sylvia's Esther when she kicked the tray
of thermometers off the table, and they broke,
and a little ball of mercury rolled

into the corner of her room, and she found it
later and picked it up and held it in her palm
because it was fascinating,

how it can divide and form two sealed versions
of what it was.
She kicked it just enough

so no one could say for sure
she'd done it on purpose.
Like the small joke I shared with the Lauren.

I am telling you this because I don't want to die
without someone knowing. I want you to go on
thinking about that white room

and the perfect placement of the red bottle.
They don't make that scent anymore.
I looked it up. You can get it on Ebay

for $500, so it's *dear*,
as they say in French. It will cost you dearly
to smell that smell again.

Duras says

even her alcoholism
was with her from the beginning,

so I must have always had this couch
and these blinds closed against the heat

and Henry who probably doesn't love me
but is just waiting for his walk and his treats

and this loneliness that is especially strong
when you turn the corner at the top

of the staircase where for a long time Henry
used to pee so also the smell of urine

is there as well, though it's faint now
after the carpet cleaning.

Something about that corner,
carrying my sons up for naptime,

their bodies already sinking into sleep,
and the terrible knowledge that lived there

that their comforting weight was temporary
which is confirmed each day now

when I round the corner on my own
to ride the stationary bike

which by definition goes nowhere
though on the screen people talk to me

and tell me I'm doing great.
I'm a bottomless well.

This is something my mother used to tell me,
which I found tactless and frightening.

You can't really get the smell of pee
out of carpet. And it took me a long

time to trust that I was really smelling it.
Duras says that when you tell a person

they drink too much,
it always comes as a shock.

I would prefer not to

The summer after Grace died,
I sat several nights on Greg and Caridwen's patio
listening to them talk about *Moby Dick*
about which Greg was writing an essay
and which I've never read and do not intend to.
But I liked learning that Melville had written
the whole book without punctuation and then later
had added the semi-colons and periods
with his feather pen. I could picture the pen
hovering above the paper and touching down
here and there like a bird catching a fish.
And it really was here and there, wasn't it,
since he wrote such long sentences?
I guess in retrospect, he didn't think they needed
much dividing. What I liked best about being there
was the way the words drifted over me
like Greg's cigar smoke and the smell of whiskey
and the way the white whale everyone's always
talking about matched the white walls
of Greg's writing studio which looks like
a gnome's house with many tiny windows.
The only thing I've ever read by Melville
is "Bartleby, the Scrivener,"
which this year I recommended to my son Ben
because he was riding the subway
one hour each way from his apartment in Brooklyn
to his job at Columbia which he hated
because all day he worked alone
on his computer at his desk.
I told him the story was funny
and an interesting commentary on work.
I told him about Bartleby saying *I would prefer not to*
when his boss asks him to do basically any task,
which is the thing most people remember about the story
since we have it printed on mugs we keep at the office.

When Ben finally read it, he was mad at me
for not telling him how sad it was.
Bartleby is sleeping in the office, quietly dying,
he said, like why can't you see that.
Yes, I replied, but what about the part
about how the two copyists, Turkey and Nippers,
are each useless for half the day but fortunately
not the same half? I would have liked to discuss
Bartleby with Caridwen and Greg,
but they were busy with the whale,
and I did not want to interrupt.
I was there because we'd all lost Grace
together, but this was something
we did not speak of, we preferred not to,
it was only in the air between us
like the cigar smoke that seeped into my sweatshirt
which when I got home, I had to wash.

I have my grandmother's veins,

which means most of the time no one knows
how much Marie is with me,

inside my right leg in particular,
behind the knee. After a while of standing,

it throbs and I have to shift
my weight and it is difficult for me to listen

to what someone wants from me
because I am standing in a garden in Brooklyn

with a pair of scissors to trim the white rosebush,
my apron splattered with sauce.

I called her Nanny, but her name was Marie.
I can't say I don't mind having her blood

running through her varicose veins
but if someone has to, I'm glad it is me.

I don't garden, but I do make her sauce
and yesterday I accidentally bought four boxes

of lemon cake mix at Trader Joe's
because I like to serve it in the summers

with berries, but then I remembered there was only
me and my husband to serve it to now that the kids

are gone, and that's a lot of cake.
I thought of Marie's roses blooming

for no one and her sauce uselessly simmering.
Marie came to this country on a ship

called the Giuseppe Verdi
on December 17, 1920. She was nine.

I don't know about you, but I like knowing this.
It adds a certain glamour to me sitting here

in these thigh-high compression hose
that I have to wear for three days

after my first round of sclerotherapy
like a cast, the doctor said, so on the third day

I stink like Sylvia's Esther
who wore her green dirndl skirt and white blouse

that she borrowed from Betsy for three weeks straight.
The hose has grown a little

damp, and my legs are now things
I lug around, lifting them in and out of bed,

you know, like all of history, like my poor Nanny
who lived before sclerotherapy,

with her husband Frank who was what they call
no good, drinking in the garage, throwing

plates, ripping the phone from the wall.
Google says sclerotherapy is a relatively

painless procedure for most people,
and I'd like to meet these most people

because I had to bite my knuckle each
of the twenty times the doctor shot

the medicine into my veins, which burns
as it travels, and still

I cried out, which then I had to apologize for,
and the doctor, whose name is Megan,

offering me a side of therapy,
said, *It's okay to cry out when I'm hurting you*,

and I said, *Thank you*, and she said,
It's so cool, watching the medicine move through the vein.

Sylvia, you can't leave your shoes!

They're patent leather!
They have that shine that almost reflects
like the look the sea sometimes gets.

I wore patent leather shoes
to my First Communion, and I could think
of little else. Church was always so endless,

which was good practice for life,
but that day, I had those shining Mary Janes
to study, in lovely contrast with my white socks

trimmed in lace. My feet were small
and declarative. *I Am, I Am, I Am!*
You left your shoes on the beach,

pointing out to sea so they would be
a sort of soul-compass when you were dead.
Good thinking!

I like to think of them there, keeping
vigil in the violet light.
Of course, you didn't do it that time,

but everywhere there are traces
of your intent.
The water was cold, and your *flesh*

winced, in cowardice, from such a death.
Oh Sylvia, I wish you would have lived,
but I do admire your self-expression.

My First Communion took place
in the chapel of the university
where my mother taught.

Because my father had also worked there
as a beloved professor
and then died like a character in a play

and left us to continue, eyes
were always sliding over us.
Especially at the moment

when we had to go up to the front
so I could receive the small circle
they said was God.

My mother and brother came up with me,
and I felt proud of the favor
God was bestowing upon me,

but at the moment I was supposed to
take the host, my brother cried out,
The Bionic Man's arm came off! And indeed

it had, it had shot off, which it did
sometimes, and we had to stop
and retrieve it,

and everyone laughed.
My mother's smile was indulgent
as it would not have been

had it been the other way around.
But that is impossible to imagine
as I am devoted to obedience,

all of my light muted, patent.
Still, I did want to be a person.
I wanted to have a very strong arm

that would sometimes shoot off.
I did have an eye that could see
far into the distance,

and what I saw was
that it would be like this
for a very long time.

Pink Moon

On the last night of class, Stephanie wondered
if Beauvoir was being descriptive or prescriptive
in her chapter on "Childhood."

I could tell Stephanie was worried about the girl
she'd been and if what she'd become was her fault
or if she just couldn't help it.

What *had* Beauvoir meant?
It was Stephanie's presentation,
and we hadn't read the chapter but we all knew

the tone Simone could take.
After class I can't hold any more words
like *ontological* or *phenomenology* in my head

or even *Being* or *Becoming* and it's a Pink Moon,
so I go for a walk with my friends,
all of them Philosophers,

and we follow the river to the university
where I first learned about Being and Becoming
and then I said maybe we should just walk

to my Childhood house, it's so close.
No one could believe it because they'd left
their Childhoods in other cities, but I like a little

knickknack shelf I can dust when I'm old
where I'll keep one of those Easter eggs you can open
and there's a bunch of small rabbits inside.

I imagine I'll get it down to show a child
who has come by selling something.
I'll say, *Oh, you're a child! I was one once!*

And the way I am now may or may not be my fault!
Then I'll show her my Childhood, right there
in the egg, and I won't even know how weird I am

as I write her a check.
Last night we came at my Childhood
from an angle. I thought we could cross

right through the playground of my grade school,
but you couldn't do that without
climbing a fence, something I'd never done

as a child so I didn't feel I could do as a woman
because Simone said I was cooked.
We had to go through the alley.

By the time we were getting close to my house,
my friends were distracted and chatting
about the Present, and I had to bring them back

to Childhood with a touch of sternness.
I showed them Cush's house on the corner,
and told them her son had a go-kart

and always flipped me off, and this family kept
their dog outside all the time on a chain.
When we got to my house, I said,

Well, this is it! like people say in movies when
their date is dropping them off,
and then there's that moment when you wonder

if they're going to kiss.
I wasn't thinking that my friends were going
to kiss me, exactly, but it did feel like

something might happen. The moon was not pink,
but it was large and full and looked like a picture.
It's called a Pink Moon because of spring,

because of pink phlox which covers the rocks
in the gardens we walk by, it's called Pink Moon
not for what it looks like but for the time

when it appears. Yes, timing is everything.
For example, this place didn't look like much
back then, but now I watch it every night.

All this time I didn't know

Gail had a brother named Tom
who died of a congenital heart condition.

I had to learn this fact from her obituary and then feel bad
about all the times I had sat on her comfortable couch

talking about my brother Tom who is alive.
And who knows when her brother Tom died?

Was he a child? How long did she know him?
The obituary says Tom's death was the reason

Gail became a therapist, so we have him to thank
for all those hours she spent listening to me,

stifling her yawns,
telling me it was okay to feel what I felt.

I also didn't know Gail converted to Judaism in 2006,
another thing that I wonder about when I wake up

and remember she's dead.
When someone dies, I think it would be best

if I don't sleep for a while at all.
Maybe this is why people sit for five days with the body

right there in their house.
But Gail's body does not belong to me.

I don't have any claim to the woman
who sat across from me every Wednesday afternoon

at three for ten years,
who wore asymmetrical sweaters and sometimes shawls,

who just last year adopted a red retriever and named her
Crimson because she already had a cat named Clover.

It is exasperating to know so little and to know
you will never know more, like with my father

who died when I was six so I only have
a few pieces of him that I have to keep going over

and my mother has grown tired of this
puzzle we're never going to solve,

so I found Gail, and now here Gail goes, dying
herself, leaving me with Crimson and sweaters,

not nearly enough information to make a life.
My mother calls and leaves me a message

that I can't stop playing.
She says, *It's okay not to be okay*,

which is something that if she'd said it years ago
might have meant I would not have needed Gail,

but there it is now, anyway.
She says I can call her back or not, but if I do,

she has a story to tell me about my son Matthew.
He texted her that he made a hot tuney for dinner,

which is what she called the hot tuna fish sandwiches
she used to make when she lived in the house on Apollo.

They'd eat them while watching
Notre Dame football, my mother yelling and calling

the players *big whiny babies*, my son delighted
to witness something usually hidden.

I don't know what to do with all the feelings
I would usually hand Gail

the way my children, even now as adults,
hand things to me, their sweatshirts, a cup

they're finished with, and I take them with a fake
resentment when really I'm glad to still be useful,

and I'm hoping Gail felt this way too.
The week before she died,

I was at the coast with my whole family,
all the characters from the stories I told Gail

gathered together. On our last night,
Ben shouted, *Whales!*

and we all went out and studied the water
and waited until they blew.

But I was greedy and wanted to see their whole bodies,
so I stayed out there the longest, watching the roll

they made in the water and thinking *that shine*
is the sea and that shine is their skin and trying

to be content with just knowing
they were there.

Dear Sylvia,

I am thinking of the tiny Alp you said
would appear in a person's eye
if they'd been to Switzerland.

Of the old woman you saw rising
in your face like *a terrible fish* and how young
you actually were but how you already knew

who you would not become.
I am thinking of how lucky it was that I ran
into Marguerite Duras on the Rue de L'Impasse

de Deux-Anges. I mean her plaque that says
she lived in that white stone building from 1946
to 1982. I like it when people live a long time

within a small perimeter because then I feel
less bad that I can't seem to move from the one
spot I've been assigned. I like having historical

friends like you and Marguerite:
you have such beautiful names, Sylvia,
like a drawer full of spoons, and Marguerite,

the name of Maya's grandmother.
I do not know why the two angels
are at an impasse,

but it is something I like to think about.
Marguerite's window looked out on a school,
which reminds me of the school where I picked up

Charlotte, who was my five-year-old charge
during the year I lived here. I did not like her.
She told me I did not have the right to sit

in the velvet upholstered chair in the foyer,
which later, after arguing for my rights,
I realized was an idiom. She told me I could not

have any of the Le Petit Écolier cookies
because they were for her, so I stood
at the kitchen window and ate them all.

This strikes me as something you and Marguerite
would have done. My friend Kate says
I need Marguerite because I need someone

with whom to grow old.
I have always enjoyed the dead,
for a time choosing only pictures of women

floating in moats to hang on my walls.
In your mirror, young girls drown.
Marguerite wrote, *I prefer your face*

as it is now. Ravaged. Is this possible?
What I like about you
is how you don't answer.

Marguerite wrote, *Very early in my life,*
it was too late... my face took off in a new direction.
Everywhere in this city, I see my new face

reflected in windows and also
the face I used to wear when I lived here,
hovering above my soft, cream-colored sweater

that I thought made me look French and like
someone who was becoming somebody else,
this person I am now.

Winged Victory

When I walked up the stairs in the Louvre
towards *The Winged Victory*,
I cried as I told my son the story

of when I brought my mom to see her
and she wept and told me
she never thought she'd get here,

and he said, *Say something cool*
I can tell my children some day,
and I said, *I miss my mother at 46.*

You are supposed to view
The Winged Victory from the side
to understand the full force

of her body leaning into the wind
on her imaginary ship, but I always see her
in memory from the front,

my mother and I climbing towards her
and her body leaning towards us.
Time is my medium and my subject.

Tell your children I said "so much time
has passed," and then I cried. Tell them
I talked with your father on the phone

and said things you found obvious,
like you are sleeping while I am trying to find
the exact spot where I stood in 1990

between Le Dôme with its shelf of fish on ice
and la fleuriste with its buckets of flowers,
and told myself in nine hours

my mother will look up at the same moon
I am seeing now.
My son says, *Mom, how can you not understand*

time zones? and I think of a movie I saw once
in which the man spends the couple's
whole nest egg and the woman tells him

that in no circumstance can he ever say
nest or *egg* again,
and I say to Ben, *c'est toi who does not*

understand time or zone or moon or corner
of boulevard and 1990.
Moi, je comprends.

Moi, j'adore how the French
always start their sentences with moi.
Moi, I speak for myself, of what I do

and do not understand.
My mother's life is nearing its end.
My friend Aileen asked me if it's difficult

never to be alone in the present,
always to be carrying the past.
I said, well, it's Anne Carson's question,

isn't it, *Where can I put it down?*
One must carry it. On doit. Il faut que.
I remember the subjunctive.

I like to boss myself around. I carry it.
It's just a slip of shadow I look through
like when you put a scarf over a lamp.

Notes

The epigraph from Marguerite Duras is from her essay, "Summer 80," included in the collection, *Me & Other Writing.*

"Mademoiselle Summer," "Dear Sylvia [When I was 32]," "Duras," "The Girl of '91," "I have my grandmother's veins," "Sylvia, you can't leave your shoes!," and "Dear Sylvia [I am thinking of the tiny Alp]" all contain references to, and sometimes direct quotes from, Sylvia Plath's *The Bell Jar.*

"Duras" references Marguerite Duras's essays, "The Smell of Chemicals" and "The People of the Night" from her collection, *Practicalities.*

"Appearance vs. Reality" references Felix Vallotton's ten woodcuts, *Intimacies,* displayed as part of an exhibit at the Portland Art Museum from October 2021 to January 2022: *Private Lives: Home and Family in the Art of the Nabis, Paris, 1889-1900.* This poem also includes a line from Emily Dickinson's poem #241, "I like a look of Agony."

"Maybe I Just Don't Like Biographies," "Infinity," and "The Woman in Love" include information from and references to Heather Clark's biography of Sylvia Plath, *Red Comet: The Short Life and Blazing Art of Sylvia Plath.*

The title of *"It is dangerous to wrap yourself in the sheet of someone else's life"* is a line from Heather Christle's *The Crying Book.* This poem also contains a mention of Kurt Cobain's sweater, which was on temporary exhibit at the Experience Music Project Seattle, WA from August 2011-April 2013 and one of Sylvia Plath's braids, which is part of the Plath collection at the Lilly Library at Indiana University.

"The Serious World," "The Woman in Love," and "Pink Moon" include lecture notes and some quoted material from *Simone de*

Beauvoir: Existentialism, Phenomenology, Feminism, a course taught by Theodra Bane at The Brooklyn Institute in the spring of 2022.

"The Woman in Love" includes a quote from Sylvia Plath from *The Unabridged Journals of Sylvia Plath* and a quote from Simone de Beauvoir's *The Second Sex* about Victor Hugo and his lover, Juliette Drouet.

"The Girl of '91" references Mary Ruefle's essay, "Pause" and Annie Ernaux's memoir, *A Girl's Story.*

"Duras says" references Marguerite Duras's essay "Alcohol" from *Practicalities.*

"Dear Sylvia [I am thinking of the tiny Alp]" references Sylvia Plath's poem, "Mirror" and Marguerite Duras's novel, *The Lover.*

"Duras," "Duras says," and "Dear Sylvia [I am thinking of the tiny Alp]" were informed by my readings for *Love, Literature, and Destruction: An Introduction to Marguerite Duras,* a course taught by Paige Sweet at The Brooklyn Institute in July 2022.

"Winged Victory" includes a quote from Anne Carson's, "The Glass Essay," and a reference to the 1985 movie, *Lost in America.*

Acknowledgments

Thank you to the following publications in which some of these poems first appeared:

Adroit Review: "Mademoiselle Summer";
Bennington Review: "Appearance vs. Reality";
Gettysburg Review: "*It is dangerous to wrap yourself in the sheet of someone else's life*," "Maybe I Just Don't Like Biographies," "The Woman in Love";
Hunger Mountain: "I Had Trouble in Getting to Solla Sollew";
The Inlander: "Not Ideal";
The Laurel Review: "Infinity," "The Serious World";
The Meadow: "Dear Sylvia [When I was 32]," "Pink Moon";
Mom Egg Review: "Winged Victory";
Pleiades: "The Gambler," "Griselda";
Poetry Northwest: "Sylvia, you can't leave your shoes!";
poets.org: "Love Poem with Staples";
Soundings East: "Duras," "Duras says," "The Girl of '91," "Dear Sylvia [I am thinking of the tiny Alp]";
SWWIM: "I have my grandmother's veins";
West Branch: "I would prefer not to."

And thank you to the many people who made this book with me, the writers from history whose work I greatly admire, Sylvia Plath, Marguerite Duras, and Simone de Beauvoir; the contemporary writers of the books I read and quoted in these poems, especially Heather Clark; my real life (and contemporary) friends who read these poems along the way and this book in several different forms, Ann Ciasullo, Kathryn Smith, Ellen Welcker, and Maya Jewell Zeller; my final readers who helped me re-envision this book's order, title, and cover, Keetje Kuipers, Annastacia Stegall, and Maya Jewell Zeller; Peter Conners, Justine Alfano, Ben Thompson, Sandy Knight, and Isabella Madeira at BOA who made this book a book; and my friends and family, especially Brad Read, Benjamin Read, and Matthew Read, for their love and support, and for allowing me to use them as "characters" in some of these poems.

About the Author

Laura Read is the author of *The Serious World (BOA Editions,* 2025), *But She Is Also Jane* (University of Massachusetts Press, 2023, winner of the Juniper Prize); *Dresses from the Old Country* (BOA Editions, 2018); *Instructions for my Mother's Funeral* (University of Pittsburgh Press, 2012, winner of the AWP Donald Hall Prize for Poetry, selected by Dorianne Laux), and *The Chewbacca on Hollywood Boulevard Reminds Me of You* (winner of the Floating Bridge Press Chapbook Award, 2010). Laura teaches at Spokane Falls Community College and in the MFA program at Eastern Washington University.

BOA Editions, Ltd. American Poets Continuum Series

No. 1 *The Fuhrer Bunker: A Cycle of Poems in Progress*
W. D. Snodgrass

No. 2 *She*
M. L. Rosenthal

No. 3 *Living With Distance*
Ralph J. Mills, Jr.

No. 4 *Not Just Any Death*
Michael Waters

No. 5 *That Was Then: New and Selected Poems*
Isabella Gardner

No. 6 *Things That Happen Where There Aren't Any People*
William Stafford

No. 7 *The Bridge of Change: Poems 1974–1980*
John Logan

No. 8 *Signatures*
Joseph Stroud

No. 9 *People Live Here: Selected Poems 1949–1983*
Louis Simpson

No. 10 *Yin*
Carolyn Kizer

No. 11 *Duhamel: Ideas of Order in Little Canada*
Bill Tremblay

No. 12 *Seeing It Was So*
Anthony Piccione

No. 13 *Hyam Plutzik: The Collected Poems*

No. 14 *Good Woman: Poems and a Memoir 1969–1980*
Lucille Clifton

No. 15 *Next: New Poems*
Lucille Clifton

No. 16 *Roxa: Voices of the Culver Family*
William B. Patrick

No. 17 *John Logan: The Collected Poems*

No. 18 *Isabella Gardner: The Collected Poems*

No. 19 *The Sunken Lightship*
Peter Makuck

No. 20 *The City in Which I Love You*
Li-Young Lee

No. 21 *Quilting: Poems 1987–1990*
Lucille Clifton

No. 22 *John Logan: The Collected Fiction*

No. 23 *Shenandoah and Other Verse Plays*
Delmore Schwartz

No. 24 *Nobody Lives on Arthur Godfrey Boulevard*
Gerald Costanzo

No. 25 *The Book of Names: New and Selected Poems*
Barton Sutter

No. 26 *Each in His Season*
W. D. Snodgrass

No. 27 *Wordworks: Poems Selected and New*
Richard Kostelanetz

No. 28 *What We Carry*
Dorianne Laux

No. 29 *Red Suitcase*
Naomi Shihab Nye

No. 30 *Song*
Brigit Pegeen Kelly

No. 31 *The Fuehrer Bunker: The Complete Cycle*
W. D. Snodgrass

No. 32 *For the Kingdom*
Anthony Piccione

No. 33 *The Quicken Tree*
Bill Knott

No. 34 *These Upraised Hands*
William B. Patrick

No. 35 *Crazy Horse in Stillness*
William Heyen

No. 36 *Quick, Now, Always*
Mark Irwin

No. 37 *I Have Tasted the Apple*
Mary Crow

No. 38 *The Terrible Stories*
Lucille Clifton

No. 39 *The Heat of Arrivals*
Ray Gonzalez

No. 40 *Jimmy & Rita*
Kim Addonizio

No. 41 *Green Ash, Red Maple, Black Gum*
Michael Waters

No. 42 *Against Distance*
Peter Makuck

No. 43 *The Night Path*
Laurie Kutchins

No. 44 *Radiography*
Bruce Bond

No. 45 *At My Ease: Uncollected Poems of the Fifties and Sixties*
David Ignatow

No. 46 *Trillium*
Richard Foerster

No. 47 *Fuel*
Naomi Shihab Nye

No. 48 *Gratitude*
Sam Hamill

No. 49 *Diana, Charles, & the Queen*
William Heyen

No. 50 *Plus Shipping*
Bob Hicok

No. 51 *Cabato Sentora*
Ray Gonzalez

No. 52 *We Didn't Come Here for This*
William B. Patrick

No. 53 *The Vandals*
Alan Michael Parker

No. 54 *To Get Here*
Wendy Mnookin

No. 55 *Living Is What I Wanted: Last Poems*
David Ignatow

No. 56 *Dusty Angel*
Michael Blumenthal

No. 57 *The Tiger Iris*
Joan Swift

No. 58 *White City*
Mark Irwin

No. 59 *Laugh at the End of the World: Collected Comic Poems 1969–1999*
Bill Knott

No. 60 *Blessing the Boats: New and Selected Poems: 1988–2000*
Lucille Clifton

No. 61 *Tell Me*
Kim Addonizio

No. 62 *Smoke*
Dorianne Laux

No. 63 *Parthenopi: New and Selected Poems*
Michael Waters

No. 64 *Rancho Notorious*
Richard Garcia

No. 65 *Jam*
Joe-Anne McLaughlin

No. 66 *A. Poulin, Jr. Selected Poems*
Edited, with an Introduction by Michael Waters

No. 67 *Small Gods of Grief*
Laure-Anne Bosselaar

No. 68 *Book of My Nights*
Li Young Lee

No. 69 *Tulip Farms and Leper Colonies*
Charles Harper Webb

No. 70 *Double Going*
Richard Foerster

No. 71 *What He Took*
Wendy Mnookin

No. 72 *The Hawk Temple at Tierra Grande*
Ray Gonzalez

No. 73 *Mules of Love*
Ellen Bass

No. 74 *The Guests at the Gate*
Anthony Piccione

No. 75 *Dumb Luck*
Sam Hamill

No. 76 *Love Song with Motor Vehicles*
Alan Michael Parker

No. 77 *Life Watch*
Willis Barnstone

No. 78 *The Owner of the House: New Collected Poems 1940–2001*
Louis Simpson

No. 79 *Is*
Wayne Dodd

No. 80 *Late*
Cecilia Woloch

No. 81 *Precipitates*
Debra Kang Dean

No. 82 *The Orchard*
Brigit Pegeen Kelly

No. 83 *Bright Hunger*
Mark Irwin

No. 84 *Desire Lines: New and Selected Poems*
Lola Haskins

No. 85 *Curious Conduct*
Jeanne Marie Beaumont

No. 86 *Mercy*
Lucille Clifton

No. 87 *Model Homes*
Wayne Koestenbaum

No. 88 *Farewell to the Starlight in Whiskey*
Barton Sutter

No. 89 *Angels for the Burning*
David Mura

No. 90 *The Rooster's Wife*
Russell Edson

No. 91 *American Children*
Jim Simmerman

No. 92 *Postcards from the Interior*
Wyn Cooper

No. 93 *You & Yours*
Naomi Shihab Nye

No. 94 *Consideration of the Guitar: New and Selected Poems 1986–2005*
Ray Gonzalez

No. 95 *Off-Season in the Promised Land*
Peter Makuck

No. 96 *The Hoopoe's Crown*
Jacqueline Osherow

No. 97 *Not for Specialists: New and Selected Poems*
W. D. Snodgrass

No. 98 *Splendor*
Steve Kronen

No. 99 *Woman Crossing a Field*
Deena Linett

No. 100 *The Burning of Troy*
Richard Foerster

No. 101 *Darling Vulgarity*
Michael Waters

No. 102 *The Persistence of Objects*
Richard Garcia

No. 103 *Slope of the Child Everlasting*
Laurie Kutchins

No. 104 *Broken Hallelujahs*
Sean Thomas Dougherty

No. 105 *Peeping Tom's Cabin: Comic Verse 1928–2008*
X. J. Kennedy

No. 106 *Disclamor*
G.C. Waldrep

No. 107 *Encouragement for a Man Falling to His Death*
Christopher Kennedy

No. 108 *Sleeping with Houdini*
Nin Andrews

No. 109 *Nomina*
Karen Volkman

No. 110 *The Fortieth Day*
Kazim Ali

No. 111 *Elephants & Butterflies*
Alan Michael Parker

No. 112 *Voices*
Lucille Clifton

No. 113 *The Moon Makes Its Own Plea*
Wendy Mnookin

No. 114 *The Heaven-Sent Leaf*
Katy Lederer

No. 115 *Struggling Times*
Louis Simpson

No. 116 *And*
Michael Blumenthal

No. 117 *Carpathia*
Cecilia Woloch

No. 118 *Seasons of Lotus, Seasons of Bone*
Matthew Shenoda

No. 119 *Sharp Stars*
Sharon Bryan

No. 120 *Cool Auditor*
Ray Gonzalez

No. 121 *Long Lens: New and Selected Poems*
Peter Makuck

No. 122 *Chaos Is the New Calm*
Wyn Cooper

No. 123 *Diwata*
Barbara Jane Reyes

No. 124 *Burning of the Three Fires*
Jeanne Marie Beaumont

No. 125 *Sasha Sings the Laundry on the Line*
Sean Thomas Dougherty

No. 126 *Your Father on the Train of Ghosts*
G.C. Waldrep and John Gallaher

No. 127 *Ennui Prophet*
Christopher Kennedy

No. 128 *Transfer*
Naomi Shihab Nye

No. 129 *Gospel Night*
Michael Waters

No. 130 *The Hands of Strangers: Poems from the Nursing Home*
Janice N. Harrington

No. 131 *Kingdom Animalia*
Aracelis Girmay

No. 132 *True Faith*
Ira Sadoff

No. 133 *The Reindeer Camps and Other Poems*
Barton Sutter

No. 134 *The Collected Poems of Lucille Clifton: 1965–2010*

No. 135 *To Keep Love Blurry*
Craig Morgan Teicher

No. 136 *Theophobia*
Bruce Beasley

No. 137 *Refuge*
Adrie Kusserow

No. 138 *The Book of Goodbyes*
Jillian Weise

No. 139 *Birth Marks*
Jim Daniels

No. 140 *No Need of Sympathy*
Fleda Brown

No. 141 *There's a Box in the Garage You Can Beat with a Stick*
Michael Teig

No. 142 *The Keys to the Jail*
Keetje Kuipers

No. 143 *All You Ask for Is Longing: New and Selected Poems 1994–2014*
Sean Thomas Dougherty

No. 144 *Copia*
Erika Meitner

No. 145 *The Chair: Prose Poems*
Richard Garcia

No. 146 *In a Landscape*
John Gallaher

No. 147 *Fanny Says*
Nickole Brown

No. 148 *Why God Is a Woman*
Nin Andrews

No. 149 *Testament*
G.C. Waldrep

No. 150 *I'm No Longer Troubled by the Extravagance*
Rick Bursky

No. 151 *Antidote for Night*
Marsha de la O

No. 152 *Beautiful Wall*
Ray Gonzalez

No. 153 *the black maria*
Aracelis Girmay

No. 154 *Celestial Joyride*
Michael Waters

No. 155 *Whereso*
Karen Volkman

No. 156 *The Day's Last Light Reddens the Leaves of the Copper Beech*
Stephen Dobyns

No. 157 *The End of Pink*
Kathryn Nuernberger

No. 158 *Mandatory Evacuation*
Peter Makuck

No. 159 *Primitive: The Art and Life of Horace H. Pippin*
Janice N. Harrington

No. 160 *The Trembling Answers*
Craig Morgan Teicher

No. 161 *Bye-Bye Land*
Christian Barter

No. 162 *Sky Country*
Christine Kitano

No. 163 *All Soul Parts Returned*
Bruce Beasley

No. 164 *The Smoke of Horses*
Charles Rafferty

No. 165 *The Second O of Sorrow*
Sean Thomas Dougherty

No. 166 *Holy Moly Carry Me*
Erika Meitner

No. 167 *Clues from the Animal Kingdom*
Christopher Kennedy

No. 168 *Dresses from the Old Country*
Laura Read

No. 169 *In Country*
Hugh Martin

No. 170 *The Tiny Journalist*
Naomi Shihab Nye

No. 171 *All Its Charms*
Keetje Kuipers

No. 172 *Night Angler*
Geffrey Davis

No. 173 *The Human Half*
Deborah Brown

No. 174 *Cyborg Detective*
Jillian Weise

No. 175 *On the Shores of Welcome Home*
Bruce Weigl

No. 176 *Rue*
Kathryn Nuernberger

No. 177 *Let's Become a Ghost Story*
Rick Bursky

No. 178 *Year of the Dog*
Deborah Paredez

No. 179 *Brand New Spacesuit*
John Gallaher

No. 180 *How to Carry Water: Selected Poems of Lucille Clifton*
Edited, with an Introduction by Aracelis Girmay

No. 181 *Caw*
Michael Waters

No. 182 *Letters to a Young Brown Girl*
Barbara Jane Reyes

No. 183 *Mother Country*
Elana Bell

No. 184 *Welcome to Sonnetville, New Jersey*
Craig Morgan Teicher

No. 185 *I Am Not Trying to Hide My Hungers from the World*
Kendra DeColo

No. 186 *The Naomi Letters*
Rachel Mennies

No. 187 *Tenderness*
Derrick Austin

No. 188 *Ceive*
B.K. Fischer

No. 189 *Diamonds*
Camille Guthrie

No. 190 *A Cluster of Noisy Planets*
Charles Rafferty

No. 191 *Useful Junk*
Erika Meitner

No. 192 *Field Notes from the Flood Zone*
Heather Sellers

No. 193 *A Season in Hell with Rimbaud*
Dustin Pearson

No. 194 *Your Emergency Contact Has Experienced an Emergency*
Chen Chen

No. 195 *A Tinderbox in Three Acts*
Cynthia Dewi Oka

No. 196 *Little Mr. Prose Poem: Selected Poems of Russell Edson*
Edited by Craig Morgan Teicher

No. 197 *The Dug-Up Gun Museum*
Matt Donovan

No. 198 *Four in Hand*
Alicia Mountain

No. 199 *Buffalo Girl*
Jessica Q. Stark

No. 200 *Nomenclatures of Invisibility*
Mahtem Shiferraw

No. 201 *Flare, Corona*
Jeannine Hall Gailey

No. 202 *Death Prefers the Minor Keys*
Sean Thomas Dougherty

No. 203 *Desire Museum*
Danielle Deulen

No. 204 *Transitory*
Subhaga Crystal Bacon

No. 205 *Every Hard Sweetness*
Sheila Carter-Jones

No. 206 *Blue on a Blue Palette*
Lynne Thompson

No. 207 *One Wild Word Away*
Geffrey Davis

No. 208 *The Strange God Who Makes Us*
Christopher Kennedy

No. 209 *Our Splendid Failure to Do the Impossible*
Rebecca Lindenberg

No. 210 *Yard Show*
Janice N. Harrington

No. 211 *The Last Song of the World*
Joseph Fasano

No. 212 *Lonely Women Make Good Lovers*
Keetje Kuipers

No. 213 *jump the gun*
Jennie Malboeuf

No. 214 *Apostle of Desire*
Bruce Weigl

No. 215 *GREEN OF ALL HEADS*
Aracelis Girmay

No. 216 *Pluck*
Adam Hughes

No. 217 *Disaster Tourism*
Rena J. Mosteirin

No. 218 *The Appendectomy Grin*
Charles Rafferty

No. 219 *The Serious World*
Laura Read

Colophon

BOA Editions, Ltd., a nonprofit publisher of poetry and other literary works, fosters readership and appreciation of contemporary literature. By identifying, cultivating, and publishing both new and established poets and selecting authors of unique literary talent, BOA brings high-quality literature to the public.

Support for this effort comes from the sale of its publications, grant funding, and private donations.

The publication of this book is made possible, in part, by the special support of the following individuals:

Anonymous (x2)
Ralph Black & Susan Murphy
Angela Bonazinga & Catherine Lewis
Bernadette Catalana
Gwen Conners, *in memory of June Baker*
Chris Dahl, *in honor of Chuck Hertrick*
Jonathan Everitt
David Fraher, *in memory of A. Poulin Jr.*
Bonnie Garner
James Hale
Nora A. Jones
Joe & Dale Klein
Keetje & Sarah Kuipers
Tony Leuzzi
Barbara Lovenheim, *in memory of John Lovenheim*
Joe McElveney
John & Judy Messenger
Dorrie Parini
Boo Poulin, *in memory of A. Poulin Jr.*
Michael Quattrone.
Deborah Ronnen
John H. Schultz
William Waddell & Linda Rubel
Michael Waters & Mihaela Moscaliuc